A Private Tour of

F ELICITA

INDEX

This edition copyright © 1997 by Richard C. Angino

All rights reserved. No reproduction of this book in whole

or in part or in any form may be made without

authorization of the copyright owner.

Published by:

FELICITA

2201 Fishing Creek Valley Rd.

Harrisburg. PA 17112-9248

Tel. (717) 599-5301, Fax. 717-599-5623

1-888-321-3713

ISBN 0-9662249-0-6

Book design by Michael Burridge, Montecito, CA

Color Separation by All Systems Color, Miamisburg, OH

Printed by Asia Print LTD. in Singapore

First Edition

Cover Picture: The Monet Water Garden at FELICITA

Back Cover Picture: The Italian Garden

Over the past ten to fifteen years, more and more garden enthusiasts have shown an interest in our lifetime endeavor of creating beautiful gardens. We have been asked on two occasions to tell our story with slides to the American Horticultural Society; we also spoke at the annual Williamsburg symposium. Our gardens are becoming the subject of numerous articles and the venue for visits by national and local gardening groups.

We are now creating a garden resort and retreat where we will be combining with our gardens a championship golf course, a state-of-the-art spa and fitness center, fine dining, quaint inn, lodges and cabins, miles of mountain trails, tennis, swimming, and volleyball Please visit — the income from our resort/retreat will perpetuate our gardens.

As either an invitation or a memento, this book gives you...

A Private Tour.

Photography: Richard C. Angino,

Charles W. Bowers & Steve Miller

F ELICITA

A Private Tour

with Richard C. Angino

T*o Alice,*

My partner in marriage, work,

gardening and life...

Alice has made these gardens

a reality.

Richard

Felicita—the Beginning

Twenty-five years ago, with our real estate
agent, Alice and I macheted our way through six
hundred feet of overgrown trees and underbrush.
To our amazement, thirty-five acres of open rolling
field spread out before us — our future Eden.

T *he First Stages*

Most gardens are planted a few trees or
shrubs at a time. For us, it was more like a hundred
trees and shrubs, thirty-five hundred bulbs, and
fifteen acres of grass over a weekend.

1

E*ntry Lane*

Except for changes in the surface (from dirt to stone to macadam), the drive leading to our home has not changed dramatically over the past twenty-five years. We kept the native oak, maple, sassafras, pine, and dogwood; and added birch, hemlock, redbud, and more dogwood. Underplantings of rhododendron, azalea, pieris, and red twig, carpeted by ferns, daffodils, and scilla, softened our woodland entry.

W*illow Garden*

The Willow Garden received its name
from the weeping willow my cousin
Dominic (visiting from Italy in 1974) and I
planted in the center of a wet area to the
west of the entry pond.

Today the entry pond and willow
garden are jam-packed with daylilies, iris,
buddleia, hydrangea, and spirea,
highlighted with forsythia, Japanese
maples, ornamental cherry, and other
flowering trees, shrubs, and perennials.

House Gardens

Front Yard:

Although we bought our land in 1972 and spent every weekend working around the "farm", we did not build our home and move in until 1975. By that time, we had already landscaped the entry lane, entry pond, Willow Garden, and Daffodil Woods; and seeded most of the previously farmed fields with grass.

The "Front Yard" originally was the northern extension of the barnyard, where a few cows, steer, and our daughter's horse, Topsy, grazed.

Every time the power failed to the electric fence, we had visitors sampling the front yard landscape.

We started with fairly common trees, shrubs, ground covers, and bulbs, dogwood, crab apples, birch, forsythia, vinca, and tulips. We gradually extended our plant palette to include Japanese maples, various conifers, azaleas, rhododendrons, and perennials. Eventually we graduated to "collecting" and adding to our collections.

In 1995 we totally redesigned and replanted the western half of the "Front Yard," adding tons of topsoil to the southern end to soften the steep slope and conceal the lower drive.

Steps and a retaining wall were built
of large rocks transported from our
mountain lands. We tucked bulbs, ground
covers, and diminutive horticultural gems
into pockets between the rocks.

Back Yard:

The relatively level "Back Yard" — consisting of two simple perennial beds, a small waterlily pool, and shade-loving shrubs planted on the north side of the home — changed dramatically in 1993.

It was transformed into an
entertainment terrace of brick with
limestone pavers, steps, walled elevated
perennial borders, and a large pond where
koi happily co-exist with an abundance of
exotic aquatic plants.

Alice's Herb Garden:

Alice always yearned for an
herb garden outside her kitchen, but the
sixty-degree slope presented a challenge.

An addition to the house in
1990 and a twelve-foot retaining wall made
Alice's dream come true. Her personalized
love-knot bench is the principal feature of
the garden.

Sculpture Conifer Bed:

Shortly after the house was built, we designed a small conifer bed in the "Back Yard" to display a birds-in-flight sculpture. Despite the major changes to the "Back Yard" in 1990 and 1993, the sculpture conifer bed remains where it has been for twenty years.

The Island Beds

Island beds we originally created in the late '70's lie to the rear or north of the "Back Yard." First they were circles with tulips followed by canna and mums. Later they became free-form beds for specimen conifers, flowering trees, and shrubs. More recently they have been reshaped, thinned, and redesigned with specialty plants.

Japanese Garden

Fred Bergman, horticulturist, collector, and propagator of rare conifers, died in 1978.

Mr. Bergman's collection was variously referred to as "One Man's Eden" and "The Secret Garden of Fred Bergman." Horticulturists all over the world knew about it but few had ever seen it.

When he died, his lifetime collection at Rara Flora Nurseries in Feasterville, Pennsylvania, went on the auction block. In 1979-1980 we purchased approximately ten percent of the Bergman collection and created an oriental garden in which to display it. Our cow pasture underwent a cataclysmic transformation!

The oriental garden created and
constructed by amateurs in 1980/81 became
a Japanese Garden in 1995 when landscape
architect Harriet Henderson lent her
professional touch. A "nice" garden became
truly something special. Harriet, who
studied for a number of years in Japan,

agreed that the Bergman specimens
displayed museum fashion should stay in
their original settings. The bright red
Chinese entry gate and mixed plantings
were replaced with a beautifully simple
structure surrounded by mature azaleas
transplanted from Daffodil Woods.

Harriet recommended and we implemented other entry changes, including substituting pebbles for grass, steps for the preexisting slope; and adding white sand and a statement rock to the base of the Japanese pine in the entry circle.

No changes were made in the entry circle of rare and unusual spruces and pines. We limbed up the magnolias and other flowering trees to emphasize the conifer underplantings.

We built a new stepping stone staircase through a peony bed to provide access from the entry circle to Harriet's new water features. Step by step, Harriet's creation unfolds. At first you see just a few rocks and water, then a dramatic stream and waterfall. Finally, powerful rapids rise, fall and roar through a series of pools.

Virtually all of the Japanese Garden as originally planted was left intact along the grassy paths to the west of the entry circle. The juniper on a standard, dogwood, simple pagoda, Bergman specimens, dwarf hemlock, Japanese maples, magnolia, cherries (underplanted with peonies, iris, nepeta, daylilies, azalea) continue as before.

We substituted large arched stones for
the small wooden bridges, repainted the
Chinese moon bridge, enlarged the grassy
area near the tea house, and added a plank
bench. Although lilacs are not typically
associated with Japanese gardens, Harriet
allowed my lilac collection to remain.

The most dramatic changes wrought by
Harriet are apparent in the eastern end of
the garden, closest to the entry drive.
In place of the watering and feeder ponds
and the stream and waterfalls leading to
them, Harriet conceived, designed, and
personally supervised the construction of
totally new rock and water features —
including bridges, waterfalls and a free-form
lower level lake. It is a sight to see.

We raided the overgrown Daffodil
Woods and stocked the new area with
specimen rhododendrons and azaleas, plus
hosta, daylilies, and woodsy wild flower
species. A few conifers were moved around,
cherries, and Japanese maples added, and
voila! Our new Japanese Garden!

The Tropical Garden

Shortly after we bought our land, we planted a two acre "labor of love" vegetable garden and orchard. For ten years we grew ten times more than we could possibly eat, gave away bushels of tomatoes, and canned and froze produce until three in the morning. Our daughter Elizabeth filled the freezers with zucchini bread.

Converting this acreage eight years
later to a swimming pool, pool house,
tennis court, pavilion, volleyball court,
and tropical garden was a decision we
have never regretted.

D *affodil Woods*

Daffodil Woods was the first of our theme gardens. We cleared trees, plowed, disked, and seeded grassy paths, and planted tens of thousands of daffodils. Over the years we added hemlock, birch, beech, dogwood, redbud, holly, magnolia, skimmia, laurel, rhododendron, azalea, forsythia, viburnum, winged euonymous, ferns, lamium, hosta,

and practically everything else that enjoys shade. Unfortunately, the daffodils are getting less and less sun and incredibly our PH 4-5 acid soil woods are becoming a neutral 7. Temperatures of minus 23 degrees over recent years destroyed all but the hardiest of the rhododendrons. The garden will be totally renovated in 1998.

Piney Ridge and Chapel Garden

For a couple of years before we moved into our new home, we spent many spring and fall weekends making four-hundred mile trips in our green Jeep pickup to and from the "Santa Claus" nursery.

There we bought Christmas trees and, on a typical weekend, we planted over a hundred pines and spruces which eventually matured into the evergreen forest we call Piney Ridge.

In 1987 we built our chapel and created a garden in memory of our youngest son, Fred.

R*ose Alleé*

In the Southwest corner of the island

beds we carved out a small section for a

rose alleé and bench.

Cherry Blossom Lane

From the beginning we welcomed
spring along a sloping walkway that led
from the house to the present Alpine Garden.
It has been variously referred to as the
Canna/Peony/Cherry/Shrub Garden because
of the existing plantings.

A*rboretum*

To the north of the island beds,
south of Daffodil Woods and the Transition
Beds, we have planted specimen beech,
cedars, and rare conifers, here enjoyed by
our German shepherd, Sushi.

M onet Water Garden

Within a few months after we bought our
Eden, we contracted for the bulldozer operator to
excavate a pond next to our future home.

As with the entry drive, we had to come in and landscape the disturbed acres. A truckload of old-fashioned perennials and ground covers were planted in spring, followed by tulips, daffodils, hyacinths and small bulbs in autumn. We then added rhododendrons and azaleas, and before long we introduced waterlilies, irises, and daylilies.

For vertical accent we interspersed a wide variety of flowering trees, willows, bald cypress, weeping white pine, oak, and tulip poplar.

I *mpressionism*

    Impressionism was the artistic rage
in the '80s, and every major city museum
exhibited Monet, Van Gogh, and Renoir.
Alice fell in love with Monet and his water
garden at Giverny.

We noticed a remarkable similarity to our pond, and in 1990, the centennial of Monet's purchase of Giverny, we added a Monet bridge, bench, chairs, and rowboat. With a few actors in period costumes portraying Monet and his family, and a charitable cause, we hosted a benefit — "Giverny Revisited." The old pond has been called the Monet Water Garden ever since.

By 1996, the Monet Water Garden had become ethereal and serene.

The daffodils, azaleas, rhododendrons, magnolias, and cherries planted twenty years ago surround the pond with gorgeous color throughout the spring months.

Underplantings of purple vinca, rare specimen helleborus, Solomon's Seal, and hosta enhance the spring bloom. Our koi from the original Oriental Garden, now two and three feet long, glide effortlessly from one end to the other.

Brilliant color from hundreds
of varieties of daylilies, hardy and
tropical waterlilies, hardy hibiscus,
and buddleia punctuates the water
garden with almost three months of
summer bloom.

A wide variety of ornamental grasses reign in the fall and extend interest through bleak winter days. All of the spring-flowering trees put on a second show through fruit and color.

One of my favorite pastimes is pruning trees and shrubs after their leaves have dropped to reveal their interesting branching structures.

Alpine Garden

This garden is one of the most popular because it makes everyone feel like Paul Bunyan or King (or Queen) of the mountain. It is a mountain range in miniature.

With a volcanic center mound and surrounding foothills, there are valleys to walk through, lakes to view up close or from afar, and mountains to scale in a few seconds. The elevations within and nearby give everyone a bird's eye or aerial view of miniature (dwarf) rock and alpine species. The real Blue Mountains in the background add breathtaking borrowed scenery.

The Alpine Garden originally was merely the northern extension of Piney Ridge. We first tried to grow walnut trees because we had heard their wood was valuable. No one told us they take a long time to mature, are not very attractive, and, incidentally, would occupy considerable space.

We abandoned the walnut grove

and in 1986 created the Alpine Garden

in its place.

Ten years after the walnut trees went and the Alpine Garden came, the miniature mountain range is at its peak. That is what some members of the Conifer Society said during their 1996 visit. Rare and dwarf pines, spruces, cedars, chamaecyparis, and junipers have begun to crowd the smaller shrubs and rock species and will have to be selectively transplanted in the future. Because most of the denizens grow very slowly, the process will probably go unnoticed. Ten years from now there will be fewer but larger and more beautiful residents.

Viewed from afar the Alpine Garden
seems "real"— an optical illusion. Up close,
the groundcovers truly appear to be alpine
meadows and rock outcrops with diminutive
flowers, berries and leaves.

Grassy paths or valleys wind through brilliant shades of red, gold, blue and green. Miniature ponds and lakes contrast with mountain "peaks" and "foothills." Rock plants and wildflowers ebb and flow. Off in the distance are the Blue Mountains.

R enaissance II: The Italian Gardens

The most recent (1993), most
spectacular, and largest (8 acres) of our
theme gardens chronicles 2200 years of
Italian gardening, from its Middle Eastern
heritage to the classical Greco-Roman

amphitheater period, on to Pompeii,
followed by the Dark Ages Cloister, through
the Renaissance and concluding with my
interpretation of a modern Italian garden.

Four terraces, seven rooms, seven ponds, three 120-foot stucco and stone walls, numerous sculptures, fountains, benches, and thousands of box, yew, arborvitae, holly, roses, and salvia complete the picture.

It all started in a cornfield.

Just as the cow pasture became the
Japanese Garden, Renaissance II belies its
humble beginnings. A veritable city arose
from a gently sloping field.

Looking back over sixteen years of horticultural experiments, I was pleased but I wanted to do something bigger, grander, different. I wanted to acknowledge my heritage and create something never done before: to present in one garden the entire history of gardens for one country.

After conceiving the idea, after reading a dozen books on famous Italian gardens, and even after building the pavilions and pergolas, I realized in 1990 that I needed expert help. This garden was beyond my limited ability, knowledge, and expertise.

Carolyn Marsh Lindsay, who was on the American Horticultural Society Board for ten years with me, recommended Harriet Henderson, landscape architect from Swarthmore, Pennsylvania. She was perfect for my take-charge independent personality. She not only collaborated with me on this Garden, but returned in 1995 to redesign our Japanese Garden.

Harriet absorbed my concept and presented some first sketches that to me were "too busy"; together we refined them and transformed ideas into reality. Harriet, Alice and I made joint decisions as to stone, color, shapes, and texture of all the hardscape.

Bill Duffy from Maryland was in town sculpting a statue for the Governor's Mansion and heard about a crazy man building an Italian Garden. His bronze sculptures now grace the pools, entry and Pompeii Garden. I absented myself from my busy law practice to design, supervise, and share in the actual planting of the gardens.

Just as with all of the preceding gardens, and the Japanese Garden to follow, I prefer to design on site and plant as I design. Although it took several years to construct, we planted the Italian Gardens in six months. We contracted for virtually all of the brick, mortar, stone and steel; my garden crew and I then planted the Italian Gardens.

The pleasure of gardening is not just to have a garden, but to design and plant one. My pleasure in gardening comes not from working at a drafting table, but from being out on the site in the sun and soil.

Reception Terrace

The Italian Gardens were designed for visitors to drive up to the Tennessee sandstone steps, climb the steps bordered by casual flowering shrubs, and walk through the entry pillars to the reception terrace for cocktails, appetizers and conversation before enjoying a play, ballet or opera in the amphitheater.

The principal feature of the reception terrace is the veil of water behind Duffy's trumpeters signalling guests that the show is about to begin.

For the grand opening benefit, Renaissance II, the wait staff wore costumes of Ancient Rome. Since then the Italian Gardens have been host to numerous benefits, galas, weddings and musical events.

The Amphitheater

A few steps up from the reception terrace is the Greco-Roman amphitheater, which is intended to depict the classical Roman period (200 BC -200 AD). Today guests sit on chairs in the grass and enjoy modern versions of classical entertainment.

The roofed pavilions and uncovered pergolas provide facilities for food and beverage service and backstage curtained dressing areas, as well as beautiful environs for sitting and socializing.

First Terrace — Pavilions and Pergolas

The view from the pavilions is spectacular.

Second Terrace — Woman Bathing

At the Second Terrace the Woman Bathing Sculpture pond is flanked by the Pompeii Garden on the east and the Cloister Garden to the west.

Pompeii Garden

The Pompeii Garden replicates the
private atrium of a patrician at the time of
the eruption of Vesuvius in 79 A.D..

Cloister Garden

The Cloister Garden exemplifies a Dark
Ages (450-1425 A.D.) garden where religious
orders grew herbs for medicine and food and
a few flowers to adorn the altar.

Third Terrace — Dancing Nudes

The Islamic Oasis Garden
(pre-200 B.C.) occupies the eastern side
garden while the chronologically extreme
modern garden can be seen at the western
edge of the Third Terrace. Between them is
a large reflecting waterlily pool featuring
the Dancing Nudes sculpture.

Modern Garden

Fourth Terrace — Synergy

Renaissance Gardens

Two late Renaissance-inspired parterre gardens overlook the Fourth Terrace where they flank the exuberantly frolicking Synergy figures dancing on the water of the largest pond.

Like children playing in the summer
spray of a fire hydrant, the Synergy dancers
are showered by multiple fountains propelling
streams of water fifteen feet in the air. These
dancing nudes depict the beauty, elegance
and exuberance of Renaissance II.

S pa and Holistic Center

Our latest project is the spa, holistic, wellness, fitness center where our guests may challenge or pamper themselves, walk the miles of mountain trails, play bocci or volleyball, or merely lie poolside.

R estaurant and Inn

Alice and I want these gardens, into which we have poured heart, soul and effort, to last long after we are gone. For this to happen, we must provide a source of revenue.

To this end, we have acquired, in addition to our spa, a small inn, a restaurant and adjoining 18 hole golf course, all adjacent to our gardens. Our guests now can share our gardens and enjoy all of the other resort activities.We hope you enjoyed this tour of our FELICITA and welcome you to come and see the gardens in person.